My First Book of CANADIAN BIRDS

Text by Andrea Miller

Art by Angela Doak

NIMBUS
PUBLISHING
NIMBUS.CA

For Antonio
—AM

To Piper and Tristan, xo
—AD

Nimbus Publishing Limited
3660 Strawberry Hill St, Halifax, NS, B3K 5A9
(902) 455-4286 nimbus.ca

Printed and bound in Canada

NB1637
Design: Heather Bryan

Library and Archives Canada Cataloguing in Publication

Title: My first book of Canadian birds / text by Andrea Miller ;
    art by Angela Doak.
Names: Miller, Andrea (Shambhala sun editor), author.
    Doak, Angela, illustrator.
Description: Previously published: 2018. | Includes bibliographical references and index.
Identifiers: Canadiana 20210384034 | ISBN 9781774710876 (softcover)
Subjects: LCSH: Birds—Canada—Juvenile literature.
Classification: LCC QL685 .M54 2022 | DDC j598.0971—dc23

Nimbus Publishing acknowledges the financial support for its publishing activities from the Government of Canada, the Canada Council for the Arts, and from the Province of Nova Scotia. We are pleased to work in partnership with the Province of Nova Scotia to develop and promote our creative industries for the benefit of all Nova Scotians.

Look up in the sky, sweetheart. A bird!

What kind of bird is it?

This bird wakes up early.

It lays blue eggs.

It's an American Robin.

This bird is like a giraffe.

It has a long neck and long legs.

It's a
Great Blue Heron.

This bird makes a sound like

a rattle.

It catches fish.

It's a
Belted Kingfisher.

This bird has red shoulders.

In Canada, it's a sign of spring.

It's a Red-Winged Blackbird.

This bird drums on trees

with its beak.

It thinks insects are tasty!

It's a Hairy Woodpecker.

This bird honks like a car horn.

Honk honk!

In a flock, it flies in a V.

It's a Canada Goose.

This bird likes lakes,

ponds, and woods.

When it's a baby, it rides on its

mommy's or daddy's back.

It's a Common Loon.

This bird lives on cliffs by the sea.

It is an amazing diver

with webbed feet.

It's a Northern Gannet.

This bird looks like a clown.

Its name means

"little brother of the north."

It's an Atlantic Puffin.

This bird hovers like a helicopter.

Its eggs are as tiny as a baby's toes.

It's a Ruby-Throated Hummingbird.

This bird is blue, white, and black.

It likes to eat acorns.

It's a Blue Jay.

This bird is the colour of a lemon.

Its song sounds like,

Sweet, sweet. I'm so sweet.

It's a Yellow Warbler.

This bird can turn its head almost
all the way around.
It's white and has yellow eyes
like a cat.

It's a Snowy Owl.

This bird doesn't mind the cold.

It lives all across Canada.

It's a Grey Jay.

Sweetheart, what's your favourite bird?